THE MANSION
LIBERATED ZONES INSIDE
THE CONTROLLED INNER CITY

Not every mansion is a playground for the wealthy.

Situated between a red brick church and a luxury condo building was The Mansion, an old Edwardian house in San Francisco's Japantown. It looked quite the desolate wreck on the outside, but inside, it was home to a young Black man newly arrived from Atlanta—and 29 houseless others. Oakland performance poet Dee Allen returns with his 10th volume of poetry, The Mansion, named in honour of his first real home in the Bay Area. The Mansion covers Allen's first 5 years surviving homelessness in San Francisco by squatting numerous buildings, whether long-abandoned or new ones under construction. In a city where alarmingly high rents, gentrification and displacements are the norm, squatting is seen as a viable means to live for the less fortunate [and resourceful].

I0617181

The Mansion
Copyright © 2025 Dee Allen.

Original Cover Art by Zinyee "Wave" Ling
Author Photo by Bill Carpenter

The fonts used are Georgia and Congenial Semi Bold
The cover font is Albertus

Gnashing Teeth Publishing
242 East Main Street
Norman AR 71960
http://www.GnashinTeethPublishing.com

Printed in the United States of America

ISBN 979-8-9898345-9-4

Library of Congress Control Number: 2024948893

Non-Fiction: Poetry

Gnashing Teeth Publishing First Edition

THE MANSION

LIBERATED ZONES INSIDE
THE CONTROLLED INNER CITY

Poems And Songs

by

Dee Allen.

For
Evan Cross,
who believes that no one
should be denied procurement of
one of the most basic human necessities:

Shelter.

Everyone has a right to a roof.

Table of Contents

On The Streets,
The Desperate & Broke Have Two Choices:

Squat
Or Rot.

INTRODUCTION

The average person believes that homelessness is "somebody else's problem", "they'll always have a steady home." Until they lose it. Through a landlord's eviction order, a bank's foreclosure notice, being kicked to the kerb by one's now-former lover—whichever way the loss comes.

When faced with lack of housing, some people have the will and ingenuity to take matters into their own hands. To actively find buildings—usually residential ones—long abandoned & empty, enter them and occupy them. This is done either as an act of personal survival or an openly political act, to raise public awareness about the lack of affordable housing. This practise, done in underdeveloped & developed regions from Lagos, Nigeria to Copenhagen, Denmark, goes by a funny name: Squatting.

My first encounter with the direct action concept of squatting was in my "Punk Rock Dude" days—the 1990s. Back in 1994, I had subscriptions to a few Anarchist newspapers: *Slingshot* from Berkeley, *The Blast* from Minneapolis and from New York City, *The Shadow*. In each issue, I would find news of a house or much larger building being occupied/used by squatters, for housing or hosting events. Some news articles spoke of full-scale evictions by police. The N.Y.P.D.-led eviction of two neighbouring squats on East 13th Street in Manhattan's Lower East Side on May 30, 1995 was the most impactful. It was a squat eviction that involved a tank and two S.W.A.T. teams. As if people housing themselves in old buildings nobody gave 3 damns about was an act of war.

Such events have a way of repeating themselves. On the morning of January 14, 2020, 30 deputies from the Alameda County Sheriff's Office converged on 2928 Magnolia Street in West Oakland. They arrived—militarised. Dressed in digital camouflage fatigues, toting AR-15 assault rifles, brought in a tank, with the intent of forcibly evicting 4 mothers and their children from a 3-bedroom house. Two months before, the 4 mothers and children moved into that house, knowing it had sat unoccupied for years. They cleaned the house and furnished it with donated furniture. The Magnolia house was not just shelter, but a statement against sky-rocketing rents in the gentrifying Bay Area. Their eviction ended 57 days of fighting over the property with Redondo Beach-based house-flipping real estate investment firm Wedgewood, Incorporated, who claimed ownership. But that wasn't the end of the story. The 4 mothers formed an organisation, similar in tactics to the anti-foreclosure Occupy Homes movement of the early 2010s: Moms 4 Housing.

In October 2001, I read an article—actually, a book review—in *Creative Loafing*, Atlanta's free weekly newspaper, on how American cities should open their doors to more "creative people". To my own understanding, the term "creative people" applied to anyone with an artistic talent, from sculptors to web site designers. Some consider writers to be among those creative people. To this day, I'd forgotten the name of that reviewed book and its author. However, I did remember a list of Top 15 artist-friendly U.S. cities the author compiled to prove his point. Number 14 was Atlanta; #15 was Detroit, dead last. At the top of that list was San Francisco.

San Francisco. While reading that list, I'd thought "Maybe I should start my life over—here."

In early November 2002, I left Atlanta for San Francisco. A single one-way Greyhound ticket—which Traveler's Aid paid 25% for—bought me a cross-country bus ride, which lasted 3 days. I made landfall at Transbay Terminal, located in a northern California city I've never visited, but heard good things about. For my first 2 nights in town, I stayed at hostels in Union Square and Fort Mason. Then I ran out of money. On my third night, a gym at a community centre in the Fillmore District, used as an emergency winter homeless shelter. It was my only homeless shelter experience in S.F., thankfully. My fourth night, however, led to my own initial experience with squatting.

One early evening trip to an ugly-looking orange office building on Turk Street not only introduced me to a contact dude who knew of a squat, but 3 social justice organisations I would later work with: Homes Not Jails, Food Not Bombs, Coalition On Homelessness. Travelling to Japantown from the Tenderloin by bus and seeing the squat in question was an adventure in itself. Being given a flashlight-led tour through a supposedly abandoned, dark old Edwardian style house from cellar to spacious attic was scary at first. But where else was I going to go? I was new to San Francisco and I didn't know a soul! At least I felt safer inside that squat than I did in a public homeless shelter with a strict curfew, terrible food and hella sketchy people! And that's not just the paid overseers!

From The Mansion to Casa Zapatista—my last squat in San Francisco's Mission District over an old abandoned Salvadorean *pupuseria*—squatting provided me with a way to overcome homelessness, albeit temporarily. My squatting experiences also provided me with adventures too good to keep to myself!

One person's illegal act is another's act of self-preservation.

Lest we forget, private property is an act of theft from somebody else and

Not every mansion is filled with the wealthy.

_____

W: 3.24

Beneath

Protect your eyes from flying pebbles.
Slip the goggles on.
Protect your palms from blisters.
Slide the gloves on.
The blacktop & grey pavement need removing.
Lift the axes, pickaxes & sledgehammers,
Activate jackhammers
And get to work
Breaking with the undesirable past.
Aching to see
The growing green future
Beneath the asphalt.

Make cracks into the dense surface.
Liberate each yard
Decolonise each acre
Of East Oakland Ohlone ground
From rock-solid
Man-made captivity
The more you swing & dredge
With construction tools.
Inching closer to
The growing green future
Beneath the asphalt.

Dump the broken pieces
Into a wheelbarrow and carry unsightly
Chunks of the past
Away from the uncovered
Site of healing.
The soft brown soil
Needs to mend itself gradually.
Rainwater & wind can aid the process along.
And so can you,
Nursing the ground
Back to proper health
In preparation for
The growing green future
Freed from asphalt.

Dig a fresh hole with a spade.
Lay down some seeds.
Reseal the hole with topsoil.
Just add water
And some fertilizer
And soon, the ground will give abundantly
What she produces for free.
Fruits, vegetables & exotic plants
Will rise, thrive & meet sunlight.
Show your little ones that food
Doesn't come from
Shelves of the marketplace.
And anyone can partake
From what collective work ushered in:
The growing green future
Freed from asphalt

And the grasp of landlords.

W: 3.19.12

Hoody
for Trayvon Martin – 1995-2012

Normally,
Whenever fog rolls in from the bay,
It devours the city whole,
Sudden temperature drop,
Everything turns grey,
Vibrant colours fade
Inside a cloudy, frigid mass—

That's the time
I reach for my hoody.
Sliding it on
One sleeve at a time
And finally, the cowl
Covering my bald head in warmth.
Fastening up the zipper—

Today,
I wear my hoody
For a different reason:

I'm in mourning.
For a boy I never met.

He wore his hoody, too.

For the last time—

The watchman's gun
Hot from firing
The watchman's mouth
Dry from lying

Casting himself in the role of a victim
Screaming "self-defence" in the faces of cops
No charges
Moments after
Premeditated chase & attack
Moments after
Tuning out

Words of caution
From the police
Telling him to
Stand down
More than once—
Yes, the watchman's protected his back
From an apparent threat to him:
A wandering boy armed
With a cellphone
And a bag of Skittles©.
The watchman's gun,
When drawn,
Was also a blade
Able to cut
An average human lifespan
Down to seventeen years.
Yes, the watchman's stood his ground,
As Florida law suggested, making
Walled Twin Lakes safe
For White privilege—

One Black father
Loses a hero.
One Black mother
Has an empty bedroom
Where her son used to be.
One Black family
Moves to defend
One of theirs
From double murder:
First, by the watchman,
Now, by the press.
First, his body,
Now, his rep.

The Amerikkkan South
Has no respect for Black life.

Today,
I wear my hoody
Because I'm in mourning.
For a boy I never met.

He wore his hoody, too.

For the last time.

W: 3.28.12

Homecoming

Back from the combatzones
Of the rest of Europe
And patriotic ticker-tape parades,
England's sons

Had no homes
To come back to
In the mid-1940s.

Military camps
Luxury flats
City hotels
Were abandoned.
Fears of air raids
By Nazi planes
Dropping bombs
Power outages
Cities blown to the bare bricks
Sent everyone running.
Crisis followed crisis:
Housing shortage.

Under nightfall's
Thick velvety cover, like
An Army battalion onto an enemy fort,
The ex-soldiers of England
Saw abandoned buildings,
Opened them up,
Took them over
And made them their own.

Huddling against a wall
In the dead cold
Wasn't an option.

Neither was languishing
For years on a public list, waiting
For the government to hand over a pre-fab cottage.

Legal paper

Fictions of "private property" & "leasing"
Never entered the equation

When the need for housing
Was greatest
Right there, right then.

Military camps
Luxury flats
City hotels
Filled in nicely
With veterans & civilians, 45,000 strong
In the post-war days.
They were better at
Re-organising society
Than Her Majesty's Kingdom,
As committees & collectives
Ran communal kitchens,
Provided first aid,
Repaired the barracks,
Ran makeshift clinics,
Opened up potential homes
For fellow dispossessed,
Defended new home-steaders
From the danger
Of ejection
Back to constant wandering
And instability
Dreaded instability
On the street—

England's sons
And Wales'
And later, Scotland's
Made good on a promise
To themselves:

Homes truly fit for heroes.
The homecoming any soldier needs.

W: 4.6.12

By Decree

Vacated—By volition
Long vacant—By volition
Break in—Your position:
Devoid of rest, devoid of shelter

Move in—Your decision
Improve it—Your decision
The courts—Their position:
"That's trespassing, not survival"

Illegal—By decree
Punishable—By decree
Without roof & walls, no one's free
True in Holland
True in England

Illegal—By decree
Punishable—By decree
Without the land, no one's free
True in Holland
True in England

W: Passover 2012

DISEMBARK

November 4, 2002: 5am:

Three days of long cross-country
Escape from the ATL
From the Dirty Dirty
From the East Coast
Ended when I stepped off
The Dirty Dog at Transbay Terminal
And touched both feet
On new, unfamiliar territory:

A West Coast city I've once read about as being
Friendly to the creative & strange.

First breakfast consumed at Denny's®
On Mission & 4th before sun broke through sky
Still ate eggs & pork sausage
Along with pancakes & peppermint tea
First two nights spent at hostels
Monday in Union Square, Tuesday in Fort Mason,
Bunk bed in either lodging,
Then empty wallet
Uncertain future I had
Made up as I went along—

Several days to seek steady lodging
Several weeks to adopt this town as my own
Several months to get to know self again
Several years to come back into my own.

All my past dreams of personal future
Didn't include
SAN FRANCISCO
But I'm here
Here to stay—

W: Easter 2012

ELLA HILL HUTCH

November 6, 2002:

Stood in a long line on Fell Street near Market at 6
The line moved occasionally before I
Passed through 39 Fell at 7:15
Signed up for a shelter bed at 7:20
Climbed aboard & rode a loaded white C.A.T.S. van at 7:45
Dropped off at an emergency winter shelter
At Ella Hill Hutch Community Centre
At 7:55
Ninety-minute wait outside the premises
Among the drunk, the smelly, the strung-out, the crazy
I was landless as they, but resolved:
"This will not be my future"
The steel doors opened at 9:30
Into the Centre
Overseers guide
Swept inside
With the houseless tide
Polished wood gymnasium floor
Clean & bare
Filled up rapidly
Nowhere left to sleep
But the wooden bleachers
Full blue backpack for my pillow
Brown leather hand-me-down trench for my blanket
Big blue suitcase, padlocked, for my headboard
Bleacher seat harder
Than the last Pantera album
Murder on my back
Lights-out at 10
Unsafe, unsettled feelings on the way to sleep—
Anyone could steal anything from me
While I'm catching Zs—
This must be what jail feels like—

November 7, 2002:

Awakened to darkness at 4:45
Aching back & shoulders from sleeping
In wooden bleachers
The gymnasium's asleep

In sync with the pre-dawn world
Nothing of mine was stolen
Unsafe, unsettled feelings persisted
Mental comparisons to jail persisted
I hated the prospect
Of controlled movement
Night after night
In environments
Like that one
Like a prisoner
And I committed no crime—

I lifted my suitcase
Out of the bleachers
Onto the gym floor slowly,
Then my backpack,
Then myself
With the ugly brown leather trench on.
Passed through the steel exit door. Never to return.

Fuck Ella Hill Hutch.
Fuck shelters.
Fuck overseers.

Neither of them
Were going to get me housed or free.

W: 4.10.12

Standstill
for Melissa Nahlen

Just imagine

Abstaining from housework
Abstaining from schoolwork
Abstaining from work for another
Abstaining from spending
Abstaining from banking

Just imagine

Bringing the flow of finance down to a slow drip
Bringing the major stores to a steel-shuttered close
Bringing yourself outside, for the streets await your
presence
Bringing that festive feeling of Carnavál to every
avenue
Bringing that sense of liberty to everyday life

Just imagine

Causing scenes of a possible future to appear when you're
Causing the normal

Functions of Capitalism to reach their proper state:
A standstill—

W: 5.25.12

Wooden Cello
for Erica Mulkey a.k.a Unwoman

She plies her trade
On the underground stage
Pretty woman sitting
Wooden cello in her lap

Just sawing away
Low-toned strains
Across wire strings
The bow begins to weave

Strands of melody
Making music skillfully

Without trying

Still sawing away
Harmonious display
Classical notes
Float above the floor

Steampunk & Goth
Listen, like they ought
Enraptured enough by
The rhythm to waltz

Inside the darkened club
Making music skillfully

Without trying

She plies her trade
On the underground stage
Pretty woman sitting
Wooden cello in her lap

W: 7.22.12

Corrective Measures

Song Lyrics
Inspired by the music of Atari Teenage Riot

Helmet visors
Spray some mace
Swing batons
Break some face

Raise up shields
Pacify the swarm
Stamp out terror
Assuming human form

CHORUS 1: Riot control
Corrective measures
Street warfare
They want combat?
They want war?
We'll take them there!

Squadcars, paddywagons
To the protest
Motorcycles on the road
Chaos in progress

Shut down the intersection
Hold down the line
Us versus them
And I'll get my overtime [pay]

CHORUS 2: Riot control
Corrective measures
Protect the system
You want slaughter?
You want blood?
Come get some!

You'll do your damage
We'll bring you pain
Hunt you & trap you
Down like wild game

If tear gas won't get you,
Concussion grenades will
Rubber bullets, tazers
Rush in for the kill

[REPEAT CHORUS 1]

[REPEAT CHORUS 2]

We are the law
You're a danger to society [4 TIMES]

W: 9.28.12
REV: 2.23.21

THE MANSION

November 7, 2002:

The Fillmore at dawnbreak:
Except for passing vehicles
On the way to and from
Slave dens
Chasing that paper,
Dead calm—

Walk from Ella Hill Hutch
Contemptible
Cinderblock shadow
Farther behind me
Hauled my worldly effects
Jansport pack on my back
Samsonite box on wheels
Led to chowline on Jones Street
Breakfast at Saint Anthony's
Tasted their poison & survived
Led to active search for shelter
I had the same luck
Finding a mate:
Slim to none
Led back to Saint Anthony's
For lunch
Poisoned again
Call me hungry
Or a glutton for punishment
Led to downtown library
Ground floor
Long queue of seats
Led to express
Internet computer
Fifteen-minute
Time limit
Fingers tickled
Keyboard
Led to Yahoo!
Led to Food Not Bombs online
Click on "California"
Scroll down to
"San Francisco"

Serving six days a week
Meeting Thursday nights at
468 Turk Street
Coalition On Homelessness
Cyberspace
Information
Led to awakened curiosity—
Hmmmmm—

Once more
Through the urban deathscape
High-crime
Higher homicide
Drug-infested
Rank from piss & shit
In some places—
The Tenderloin—

Found it.
Three blocks from the library.

468 Turk Street. It wasn't hard finding
The only building on the block
Mustard yellow
Sunkist orange trim.
Doorbell button pressed
Electric buzz opened
Ugly iron-grated door.
Door knob turned
Hiked up one flight of stairs
With my luggage
Three hundred pounds of Black & obese
Waited for me at the top.
He might stomp my ass—

Big Willie. His kindness betrayed his
Intimidating size.
I asked Big Willie
About the Food Not Bombs meeting.
Big Willie escorted me to
A room hosting a
Homes Not Jails meeting.

Facilitator L.S.
Sent me to the reception area.
Noticing that I had my luggage
And nowhere to go,

A cute Vietnamese desk clerk
Gave her friend a ring.
From the other end of the telephone receiver,
Salim instructed me to watch out for
A tall man with an Afro & dark blue trench
At the Food Not Bombs meeting:
My designated guide for housing that night.

After the meeting ended,
I met the stranger Salim described:
Tall man. Afro. Dark blue trench.
My first friend in San Francisco: Ralowe.

Almost stray dog style, I
Followed Ralowe to a bus stop
Between Geary & Van Ness &
We entered through the back door of
The crowded #38. My first MUNI bus ride.
Disembark at Geary & Fillmore. Enter Japantown.
Left on Fillmore. Trot three blocks north.
Left on Sutter. Trot down a dark, deserted driveway.
Chainlink fence swung open.
Enter sidedoor. To an Edwardian Gothic
Wreck, nearly one hundred years old, closed to
The public for unspecified years, *sans* electricity.
Ralowe led me up a spiral staircase
In the pitch black indoors.

Second floor. A long, piercing
Strip of halogen light
Lacerated utter darkness. Ralowe & I
Met Salim & Katherine. With his Maglite©,
Salim gave Katherine & I an impromptu tour of this
Large, archaic house of yet-to-be-questioned history.
Basement: Frightening, but huge.
First floor: Save for one well-lived in, empty rooms.
                Kitchen with functional stove and refrigerator.

Third floor: Spacious attic. Three rooms unclaimed.

Back to second floor. Katherine, somewhat frightened,
Decided not to stay. Being new in town, I stayed.
Salim provided me with a couple of
Tattered blankets & a room. Personal
Inner sanctum:
No door, no lock,
One window boarded up, one window intact.

I laid down my backpack & suitcase
In that ice-cold bedroom, kept my caramel
Brown leather trench on, took off my black leather
Timberlands©, crawled under both tattered blankets,
Snacked on a chocolate croissant and
Thought on the way to needed sleep:

"This squat. Any squat. The soultion to homelessness
                    is right here."

How did I repay
Salim & Ralowe for providing me
Shelter miles away from my family?

By giving my doorless room life,
Enjoying hot showers in the morning,
Dinners & desserts by candlelight,
Bringing in four more heads from the outside,
Also new to the Bay: Ruth, Remy, Russell & Brandon,
Stocking second floor closet shelves with
Tools, candles, matches, first aid kits, blankets
                    & water jugs,
Stocking the dumb waiter with food
Gathered from soup kitchens & grocery giveaways,
Giving tours of all four floors to new people
Either passing through or staying for the long haul,
Teaching the new ones the secret squat knock as easy
Identification for us old heads,
Doing dumpster-dive runs near midnight
As Japantown & Fillmore were off to
The sleep of the righteous,
Writing a short note of thanks before
Leaving the squat for work & residency at the Broadmoor Hotel.

December 2002:

Housekeeper
For the Broadmoor:

Last hired,
First fired.
Just two weeks of work.

Room eviction.
Shown to the lobby's glass front door.
Days before Xmas.
At least I was paid
My severance cheques. First. Last.
At least I'm away from that cheap
Vodka-sucking Ghanaian drunk.

One cold night at an S.R.O. hotel on O'Farrell
The Ghanaian recommended
[He probably drank up his sorrow there, too]
Two rainy nights at a hostel on Mason
The former Hotel Virginia
Were steeping stones
Downward

To the same long queue of desperate,
Sad houseless, all dirty clothes & dirty luggage,
Corner to front door at 39 Fell.
I came goddamn close to inching to the front door
And begging some counselor to book me a
Shelter bed. An epiphany
Helped me to remember
The grand old house
On Sutter, between Steiner & Pierce, between
A solid brick Black Protestant church &
Expensive luxury condos, between
The wealthy & the pious, where the rebellious stayed
Living on the down low—

I had a place to go on Xmas Eve after all—

Xmas Eve 2002:

Me and my luggage
Boarded the 38 bus, back door
From Geary & Van Ness. Geary & Fillmore: my stop.

My late-night homecoming.
Probing, stumbling my way through darkness
From back door on the first floor,
Up the spiral staircase to my old room on the second.

Salim wondered what I was doing back.
I gave him my short, sob story about my tenure at
The Broadmoor, only to be fired & evicted without good reason.
To that, Salim replied, "Make yourself at home."

January 2003:

Remy & Old Man Dave,
Our downstairs neighbour,
Worked together on repairing the house's
Electrical wiring. When repairs were done, one
Flick of the switch—
Let there be lights—And there were plenty—

The harsh fluorescent lights above my room
Made it easier for me to see my dinner & apple juice
And read "The Real Bettie Page."
No more candles.

Returning home one Monday night, Sutter Street
Was under police occupation. Flashing
Red & blue lights, three black & white
Squadcars—dead giveaway. The officers had
Questioned my eight squatmates, sitting in front of
Our house, their backpacks & sleepingbags
Lined up like little soldiers in our driveway.
Sapphire & I witnessed the eviction from a safe distance
Across the street.

This was panic time. This spelled the end of
A sweet squat
Big enough to be a mansion.

Sapphire & I had to tell our crew
At the Redstone Building how our house was lost—

Re-entry
Into that old grand house on Sutter Street
As a group:

February 1, 2003:

Three young squatters
Used the tools of carpenters
To re-open the sweet squat
Big enough to be a mansion.

Into the attic we went
To retire for the night. Three in one room. Into our
Sleeping bags. Rest up for a
Homes Not Jails action, set for the next noon.

We awakened
To surprise guests:
The S.F.P.D.

With a snug little van outside.
Just the three of us. My first arrest.

February 15, 2003:

The incessant
Pouring rain
Wasn't an impediment
For four squatters & a dog,
Determined to get back inside
Their evicted home.
All the usual entrances
Shut tight.
All that for an old house
Depopulated on purpose
Bought by U.D.R.
For demolition.
Shut tight in
All the usual entrances
Save one:
Second floor window
To my old bedroom.
We scaled up
The fire escape,
My old bedroom window:
Shut tight also.
There was a little remedy for that:
Dark wool seater
Encasing a blunt object
Shattered wet glass
When swung—

September 2003:

A rag-tag team of travellers & rebels
Made a cross-town journey from The Railroad in
Noe Valley & paid a visit to that sweet squat
Big enough to be a mansion.
One blond, bearded Hippy traveller likened the old
Edwardian spread to the one in "Fight Club".

With pocket flashlights & carpenter's tools,
Doors were re-opened, locks were changed,
The old house was liberated again. It felt
Nostalgic, calming to sleep surrounded by its walls.
Our team broke camp together in the attic,
Flashlights gave light for a little while. The team
Spoke of plans & ambitions for the house, whilst I'd
Shut both eyes, laid flat & retreated to memories.

Two days later,
The same carpenter's tools
In different hands
Changed the locks & locked the doors and windows,
Depriving us of home yet again—

Re-entry
Into that grand old house on Sutter Street
Alone:

October-November 2003:

The after hours
Adventure of entering
That sweet squat
Big enough to be a mansion
Had the thrills
Siphoned from it.
During the last dozen times,
It became
A simple nightly
Survival tactic at best.
I felt less like
Spider-Man or James Bond
And more like
Another desperate houseless man.
I needed somewhere to
Rest my head at the end of the day.
I chose to do it in the old neighbourhood:
Japantown.

The old open driveway
Now had a chainlink fence-door
Blocking the path. Imposing. Locked. Chained.
Climbing over the fence-door and down were
The only times that Spider-Man feeling returned.

The iron fire escape in the back
Always provided a path.
My old second-floor bedroom window,
An easy entrance.
Just slip into the hole made
Damn near a year
Earlier—careful not to cut
My fingers on the protruding
Glass shards on the frame—and
I'm at one with the dark interior.
Scramble up the narrow stairwell
To the attic and chose
One of the rooms in which to
Unfurl my sleepingbag & pass out.

Every night's exactly the same:
Always quiet.
Always dark.
Always too
Vast & empty.

November 2003:

I scaled up the fence,
Crept to the back of the old house,
Used the darkness to my advantage,
Scaled up the fire escape to my
Old second-floor bedroom window
One last time.

Next window pane.
Locked up tight.
Damn. No way in.
No tools for making an entrance.
Resignation.

I took all my steps again
In reverse.

Just as I was
Almost over the fence,
A bright beam of light
Shined on me

From a flashlight
Of a security guard
From the condos next door! Shit!

He ordered me to freeze. I did
The complete opposite. I
Threw my sleepingbag down on the driveway,
Jumped off the fence with a full backpack and
Ran down Sutter, continued down Fillmore.
Carried my sleepingbag, ran with the late night wind.
Ran against possible police capture.

Hardly a wink of sleep that night—

June 2006:

It felt good to be in the old neighbourhood—

Travelling to a vegan potluck at a house
On Sutter Street on foot gave me
A chance to see my first home in the city again.

In between a
Solid brick Black Protestant church &
Expensive luxury condominiums was

A construction site.
Or rather, a destruction site.

Resting beneath a Bobcat©
Bulldozer,

Broken stones,
Wooden slats,
And grey dust—

If that pile of rubble
Could tell stories,
It would

Of a sweet squat
Big enough to be a mansion.

An Edwardian Gothic spread,
Built after the 1906 earthquake.
A mansion that housed

Battered women once.
Long de-populated
In high-end Japantown.

Re-opened by
The Autonomous Collective
A few months before
The Dirty Dog brought me into town.
The rooms of that grand old house

Had life again
For six months.
Re-populated by
Thirty souls
Who sought shelter despite
Increasing rents,
Waves of affluent
Asswipes.
I arrived for its
Last two months.

Tumble of broken stones,
Protruding, splintered wooden slats,
Mound of grey dust—

All that remained of
A safe haven for the poor.
My old home in the city
And you never forget your first.

Not every mansion is
Filled with the wealthy.

W: 11.12 to 6.13

Stay Silent
for Matt Duran & Katie Olejnik

You're the latest
Catch in the federal dragnet
To your dismay.
You're summoned before
A cold, insinuating
Set of faces.
Take a seat
On the stand
And you're welcomed
Like the worst possible criminal.

Barrage of questions
Fly at you
Rapid-fire in
Their secret proceedings.
Seated target has
No line of defence:
Barristers aren't allowed.
Witnesses are forbidden.
So you do
What heart advises:

Stay silent.

Summoned before the
Grand accusers again.
Take a seat and
Be a target again.
Barrage of questions
Dead aim again.
Probing for names
And identities
Familiar to you.
Digging for weakness
Gripping fear
On your part.
The accusers
Count greatly on your
Capitulation, cooperation

Collaboration & implication
Of nearest & dearest.
You choose again to
Stay silent.
Taciturn rebel
Charged with contempt
By a jury of no peers.
You feel nothing
For the court
But contempt.
As your punishment,
Buried alive
In grey concrete,
Reinforced steel door,
Digital lock, alone.
Even this
Won't loosen your lips
Make you
Breathe a word
Whole sentences and
Destroy a community.
To do so would
Help the witchfinders.
We know how that shit worked for
Early Massachusetts
Puritan culture.

There'll be no
Drownings or hangings.
Not on your watch.
Keep those lips sealed.
You saw nothing.
You heard nothing.
You breathe nothing.

The quiet can be powerful.

Stay silent.

W: 10.16.12

Ghost Dance

Song Lyrics
for Doug Benner

As long as the bright sun rises
And the gentle wind blows
As long as the old tree rises
And the green grass grows

These sacred grounds are ours always
Core of our long-held belief
But strangers come to take it all away
Return to us as we glide our feet

CHORUS 1: Ancestors
         You are our only salvation
         Ancestors
         Shield us from devastation
         Ancestors
         Deliver us from their debasement
         Ancestors
         Shield us from forced displacement

Now we need you more than ever
Your spirits will protect us
From wasi'chu who wish to sever
Our lifeways and disrespect us

Lakota—sustainers of these lands—
Shunkawakan, lakes, earth we nurture
Our feet shall move with you in this [round] dance
To spare our people, save our future

[REPEAT CHORUS 1]

CHORUS 2: Three days
         Last chance

         Three days
         We glide

         Three days

We dance

Three days
Old souls on our side

W: 12.12.12

Invertebrate

Invertebrate creature,
Lamest one.
Your condition is spineless.
Your position is weakness.
Your name is Progressive.
Your name is Liberal.

Invertebrate creature,
Servile one.
Obedience is your watchword.
Resistance, "a dirty word".
Your name is Progressive.
Your name is Liberal.

Invertebrate creature,
Passive one.
Capitalism is your comfort.
The greener kind won't upset the apple cart.
Your name is Progressive.
Your name is Liberal.

Good citizen
Good intentions
And nothing to show
For them but
Bad tactics
That won't change shit,
Though the situation's
Appearance will change.
Questionable logic
That gives support
To a decaying,
Dying system
Even the Right
Would fight to save.
Content to keep crawling.
Content to keep kneeling
Before the feet of leaders.

Algae

Has more spine than you—

You wish for peace.
I want that, too.
You have good intentions.
Good for you.
Conscious about the environment.
Good for you.
But are you conscious
Of the immediate environment?
Of this neighborhood? Of this city?
Sliding on in, oblivious, totally
Silent on a burning fact, a
Violent change so painfully obvious as
The new condo tower slowly
Being built, climbing up the lowest
Sky, story by story. Obvious as
The poor family driving away in a
Moving van, with their lives
Stored in taped, marked boxes, to
Parts unknown, high-priced
Out of the apartment they used to call home:

You gentrify
My block.

W: 5.21.13

REDSTONE

February 2003:

Named in honour of
The material it was
Built from besides
Cement, paint and steel. It was
A temple to labour in the Mission District,
Leftover from the Great Depression, an age
When labour unions actually
Organised their workers to fight for themselves—

Redstone. It was

A blunt object workers used to
Chuck at lines of cops & scabs during workplace strikes.

Redstone. It was

Three-story
Thirty-day
Temporary home
Transitional crashpad
Between The Mansion & the next great squat.
Host to a second-floor
Office dangerously close
To the elevator, shared with
Indymedia & Whispered Media, where
My collective & me
Slept on beat-up, second-hand
Couches & dirty, tacky carpet,
Stored our belongings rescued from that
Construction crew at The Mansion after the raid,
Prepared our meals in a microwave & a rice cooker,
Held our meetings in the main computer lab,
Brought back delicious treats from the dive
Into La Victoria Bakery's dumpster,
Gave Theatre Rhinoceros hell for loud rehearsed yelling.

Redstone. It was

Where my collective & me
Were ejected from, by way of
Indymedia's consensus decision. Not a soul blocked it.

W: Gay Pride Day 2013

Reverence

After the heart ceases to beat,
The breath leaves,
The limbs won't move,
The vision fades to total black,
A person's
Name, reputation, accomplishments,
Nature, charm, memories shaped with you
Develop their own currency.
Worth our reverence
And flowing tears.

Then, a little question nags at you:

"How will I be remembered?"

Our reverence,
Best to be spent
On those who
Walk among us still.
Bearing names still remembered,
Holding reputations still being built,
Natures many already accepted.
Receiving their charms as gifts to the heart,
New memories & accomplishments
Twisted into shape
When you're together.

Then, little solutions stay with you:

Respect the dead. Celebrate the living.

W: 9.1.13

THE THORN

March 2003:

1.

Some
Muscular, boyish,
Freckle-faced
Homes Not Jails
Volunteer,
Whose name still
Escapes me today,
Handed me a
Couple of keys:
To the front gate
To the front door
To a former
Art studio.
Or should I say
A series of them?
Beauty to behold—

Ceilings higher
Than Haight-Ashbury
Was in 1968.
Roomspace wider
Than my younger
Fat cousin's waistline.

The best
Birthday gift in years.

I lost The Mansion.
I gained The Thorn.
Protruding thorn on a stem
Called Rose Street, off Upper Market—

2.

At another of their Wednesday night meetings,
Homes Not Jails asked me if
I could put up a young White couple,
Evicted from their Haight-Ashbury apartment,

At my squat. Out of a need to fill rooms,
I accepted them.

It took Chris & Tonya
An entire night to explore all the rooms of
A protruding thorn on a stem
Called Rose Street, off Upper Market—

Chris & Tonya took one of the front rooms.

Amenities that awaited them [and me]:

No water. Bone-dry, non-working toilet & sink.
Plenty of electricity. Wide floorspace
Covered in dried guano.
The pigeons flew near the ceiling.

Back rooms—still vacant—

3.

It was an adventure in itself:

Exploring all the rooms of
A protruding thorn on a stem
Called Rose Street, off Upper Market.

In one of these spacious rooms,
Chris & Tonya found
A nickle-plated
Nine-mil Glock. Probably loaded.
The couple had shown me
Their small arms discovery. Fear ran through me.
Because of this, the three of us
Held our first house meeting.

The three-way chit-chat
Led us to instituting, for our new home,
A no-weapons policy. Especially guns.
At the end of the meeting, we
Also decided that one of us
Should dispose of the gun. Elsewhere.

Tonya refused to do it. Chris refused, too.
By default, I was the one to do the disposal work.

Outside, fear ran through me still
Holding a machine designed to kill.
Away from home, I found
The first rubbish bin I saw, on
Some lonely Hayes Valley corner.

I threw it in, the source of my grief,
Nickle-plated nine-mil,
Wrapped in a black bandanna.

March 19, 2003:

Coalition On Homelessness
Asked for volunteers to be
Houseless guides to visiting
Kansas University students.
I stepped forward. And accepted their offer.
It was the easiest $50 I ever made.

For one day, my
Out-of-town guests
Followed me around & took notes
Of my daily life, young and Black,
Houseless in San Francisco.

Starting point of our tour:
A protruding thorn on a stem
Called Rose Street, off Upper Market.
To me, it was home.
Erin, Ben & Joe
Midwestern, White & young
As privileged as they come
Were led through labyrinthine
Corridors into oversized rooms
That could house 8 at once.

Next stop: 39 Fell.
The three Midwesterners bore
Witness to the long, sad line of desperation
I was once part of, ended at
The front registration desk inside.
Flowing like water streams, most of the day,
Shelter referrals. Vacant beds.

Next stop: Starbuck's, inside the Hotel Whitcomb.
A place to get free cups of hot water.
I provided my guests with lemon tea bags
And Turbinado packets.

Next stop: UN Plaza Café.
San Francisco grey sky

Began pouring cold rain.
Our crew was wet & starving.
Only dry, free area in sight:
The blue canopy above
UN Plaza Café. Closed.
Food Not Bombs huddled
Under it to serve free, hot
Vegetarian food, as always. Soup & bread hit the spot.

Next stop: anti-war march.
The roving protest against Bush's
Planned invasion of Iraq was
Bigger than usual. Louder. Angrier.
On a whim, Erin, Ben, Joe & me
Traded one crowd for another.
We left Food Not Bombs' serving and
Joined the march down Market,
Despite getting drenched. Fuck the rain.
Fuck rush hour. Time to stop a war.

Three miles in a steady
Downpour, we marched.
Through three busy major
Streets & a secondary downpour
Of chants, we marched.
Past irate cops, we marched
Against an international bloodbath
Only Fox News & P.N.A.C. wanted.

Anti-imperialist
Procession
Followed a flatbed pickup truck,
As rain continued to pour.
All picket signs, banners, voices of discontent.
The people's demand,
Shouted out loud,
Repeated the world over:
"NO WAR IN IRAQ!"

Stopover: 24th and Mission.
The procession filled in
The space between McDonald's & B.A.R.T.

The pickup truck parked in the street sideways,
Served as a temporary stage.
Three messengers with bullhorns
Delivered the same ominous news:
Bombs over Baghdad
U$ first strike
Shock & Awe
Around the world:
"THE WAR HAS BEGUN!"

Shock & Awe has spread to the Mission.
Afterwards, collective rage. That spread to me, too.
Second conflict in the Gulf. Threat to Amerikkka's
                          young.
Time to bring a war home.

Banks & P.G.&E,
Front windows smashed
Economic damage
Fast-moving shadows
Outrace approaching cops
In the first hour of war.
I lost one of my guests,
Joe, somewhere in the raging
Anti-war procession, Erin, Ben & me had
Found him, nearly snatched up
By cops eager to grab any collar.
The four of us disappeared from Mission & 22nd,
Where the first arrest was made.

Next stop: Safeway.
Like some angry wolf, my stomach growled.
Nourished on itself, with canines only I felt.
The four of us grabbed snacks & dinner items.
My treat. A vegetarian panini & mango smoothie
Had my name on them. The food stamp card, E.B.T.,
                          a lifesaver.

Back to The Thorn.
The tour ends. Full circle.
Visiting Kansas University students
Had to return to a church each night for

Their lodging, after a day with their houseless guests.
But not Erin, Ben & Joe. These three Jayhawks
Were so intrigued by my massive flat. I gave them
A room with a sliding glass patio-style door, 2
Floodlights mounted on the upper wall & a
Working microwave on the floor.
Somewhere they could warm food, dine & sleep.

Now they had plenty to write class papers about—

Early April 2003:

Noises from the rooftop
Above my room—
Sounds like footsteps
Awakened me
Prevented me
From sleeping all morning through—

Beyond sick and
Tired of the dry
Crustiness underfoot—
Hardened pigeon shit—
I visualised cleaner
Concrete floors.

With a pail on wheels filled
With degreaser & store-bought tanks of water,
A mop, a broom, a dustpan,
A scraper blade on a long stick
And a plastic wastebasket,
Alonzo, another brother, originally from Las Vegas,
And me had put in some sweat equity
                on that floor.

Scrape. Sweep. Dump. Mop. Squeeze. Dry.

The building owner & 2 construction workers
Walked in on us. Total wide-eyed, jaw-dropping
Shock on 3 faces.

Whilst he appreciated the work Alonzo & me
                did on the floor,
The building owner gave us
Twenty minutes to leave *his* building.
Tonya & Chris were the last to get the
                eviction news.

Another rent-free home lost—

March 2014:

The Thorn I knew
Still stands on Rose Street, off Market,
Across from Zuni's.

The shell, anyway.

The last technological
Gold Rush in the 2000s—
Biotech--changed parts of San Fran
And with them, my old squat.

1908 stable house—
A piece of obsolescence
Attached to new school
Steel and blue glass opulence—Eight floors worth.

I wear black to recall
The loss of a home that kept me off the street,
That I wanted to provide to others in my situation,
A safe haven that was taken from me.
Remembering the loss of a home
I was forced out of.
A time to mourn. A moment for tears.

W: 9.13 to 3.14

Ambassadors
for Bruce Allison

In the centre of any metropolis
Ubiquitous as the shops
These strangers in odd vests & hats—
Assuming the roles of cops.

"Downtown revitalisation".
"Business improvement".
"Special services".
"Community improvement".
Names tossed around to describe
What these strangers do, but they're
Commonly known as "ambassadors".

Sometimes with dustpans & brooms,
Sweeping sidewalks clear of trash.
Sometimes with cusswords & force,
Sweeping sidewalks clear of gathering
Houseless, treated like trash.
Sometimes as janitors,
Keeping the concrete clean.
Sometimes as traitors
To the fellow broke,
Keeping the invisible poor quite invisible.

Forbidden to panhandle,
Play music,
Sing songs of a
Hard knock life
On cold concrete,
Post flyers,
Sell homemade wares,
Crowd the sidewalk
With scuffed-up bags
And leashed dogs,
Dig through trash
Bins for discarded
Aluminium cash,
Sit or lie anywhere—
Forbidden to be

Human in plain sight—

"These downtown streets are made
Only for shopping. Clean, safe for tourists."
Ambassadors' visitations
On houseless populations,
Conducted on the daily
With this mindset.
The same mindset
That torn down a massive
Tent city in Fresno. Central Valley safe ground
Rendered unsafe—

In the centre of any metropolis
Ubiquitous as the shops
These strangers in odd vests & hats—
The harassment never stops.

W: 12.5.13

Masterpiece
for Alina Popa

It's taken you
Literally years to
Conceive and create
A living work of art.

Working with soft,
Raw, organic material.
All access to
The right tools
Made of heavy iron,
Not to
Hammer away or chisel off,
But to
Lift up and down.
Minutes on end.
Days on end.
To steadily sculpt
Your dream structure,
Which could rival
The work of more
Legendary artists
To build

Broader shoulders,
Stronger back,
Fuller chest,
Thicker arms and thighs,
Rippling abs,
Healthier calves:

Your masterpiece.

Additional work is done
To your structure.
The task is never complete,
But you unveil your evolving work
Proudly on display.

Some men would run away

Out of fear.
Some women would turn away
Out of puzzlement.
What they see is
What they don't get.
That only shows
They can't handle
Your labour of self-love,
Your masterpiece:

A whole lot of woman.

Your muscles
May have already defined you,
Most of the world
Have admitted disapproval of your art,
But never forget:

You have achieved
Physical perfection.
You have
The body beautiful.
You are feminine.
You are desirable.

Let no one
Tell you different.

W: 1.13.14

Shining Star
for Amiri Baraka – 1934 – 2014

I don't have too much
Time just sitting around counting stars.
I have to be in another
Part of town to accomplish that.

Alone, hiking around a dark
Bernal Hill with a flashlight,
I can see the stars above much
Better than I could in the Mission's
Drastic urban change below.

One shining star
Was missing from the ebony sky.
The hole it left is untraceable.
I've followed that star's
Brilliant shine for over twenty years.

Caught by its halogen-like luminence,
That star inspired me to craft
Poems that kill, wrestle cops in alleys,
Make me feel and be me, shake off to the
Best of my ability *madness and dead skull songs,*
Transform my home-spun writing into implements
That splinter fire, encourage me to *keep, keep*
Throwing hard, keep on punching and never
Let mine enemies *dodge* once,
Use my scrawled verses in a daily struggle
That transcends class, *as my beautiful*
People with African eyes, nose and arms
Have for centuries, *wanting sun* aplenty
In a vast land where *heathens think*
Fascism is civilization and *Luxury is* everyday
Comfortable ignorance.

In the slums, projects and blue-collar suburbs,
There's always *a railroad made of* hella
Human bones—Black ivory, Black ivory, Black ivory—
When this situation worsens, *lovers and warriors*
And their sons should *unite* and come out

Fighting its conditions, even when *the devil*
With the blue uniform & badge shows up in a hot
Harlem minute—*IT'S NATION TIME!*
IT'S NATION TIME! IT'S NATION TIME!

One shining star
Is missing from the ebony sky.
The hole it left is untraceable.
That star disappeared, joining
Shining stars of the past in the endless void,
A parallel sky of sorts.
Like others that came before, that star unique

Newark street kid
Beatnik
Kawaida
Communist
Not anti-Semitic
Anti-Zionist

More *spirit* than *ghost*
Born Everett Leroi Jones
Renamed Blessed Prince

Inspired me to pick up the pen
And fill notebooks with
Words that still move the people.

W: Martin Luther King Birthday 2014

GREENLAND

July 2003:

Three-man
Search team—

A grand old dame of a
Boarded-up church in Alta Vista—

We had a desired spot. We had a plan.
We had the manpower. We had the tools.
What we sorely lacked was
Graceful execution of the plan.
Each time we'd gotten closer to entering
The boarded-up chapel,
Neighbours would watch us. Thinking of us as vandals.
Far less graceful was
Being chased down Turk Street,
Against the muggy summer night, angry
Neighbourhood Black youth running behind us—
The irony in this: I'm Black, too—

So much for Plan A. Tony's plan sounded great
In conversation—

I told Tony & our train-hopping comrade Trashcan
About another site I'd visited twice:
A house on Central Avenue opened by H.N.J.
Deep, dark green like forests north of the Bay,
Bright, healthy green lawn, seemingly untouched,
No electrical power, just running water, one storey.

We hid from our pursuers & rested for the night inside

Plan B.

W: 4.27.14

OAKTREE MANOR

July 2003:

In the afternoon sun,
We toiled away
In the backyard of a Victorian home
Near Panhandle Park
Long condemned

Pruning branches from trees with a saw,
Trimming bushes with shears,
Scooping up trimmings with a rake,
Shoving them & scattered trash
Into large Hefty© bags,
Propping a small ladder behind the back door
As steps, since the back porch was
Missing, probably dismantled long ago—

Before the eyes of a few curious neighbours,
We toiled away
In the backyard and
Inside the manor—
The unlivable suddenly
Made livable again
Because of my houseless crew & me—

Like colonies of bats,
Squatters do dirt most
And live for the
Dark vastness of night.
Unlike those
Winged rodents,
Squatters can do
Amazing things in
The daylight, too.

W: 6.2.14

Derelict 2

Song Lyrics
Inspired by the music of Unwoman

The news just reached my building
The landlord just raised the cost
Of my staying here month to month—
Into panic, I'm tossed

I'm forced to make a tough choice
Between food and rent
There's no harm in needing to eat—
Into the cold, I'm sent

Expelled from refuge, when I walked out that door
Seeking shelter, I've been here before

Return to a life I dread
Wandering the city streets
Return to being a hated pariah
Everyone mistreats

Return to splitting life in half
Between streets & rooms of friends
This longing for space to call my own
Never fucking ends

Stable living not found, this I can't ignore
Missing shelter, I've been here before

A derelict again [3 TIMES]

W: 6.6.14

THE RAILROAD

September-October 2003:

For one month, I made my home
On Chattanooga & 21st,
In the Valley that is Noe,
Amidst proud painted ladies.
Not the ones that stand on
Tenderloin sidewalks at night
For sexual favours. Not those.
Restored Victorian/Edwardian
Painted houses. Yup, those.

Townhouses, architectural
Twins, two stories of plain white
Emptiness. At first.
Unfilled on top, unfilled on the bottom.
Tony, me, Jolene, Zachariah, Jamaica & some others
Stayed on the bottom floor.
Sliding glass patio door in the back, always unlocked,
Gas & water worked, electricity didn't.
Hot showers in the bathroom,
Hot meals from the kitchen stove,
Warmth flowing from the heating vents.
In the nocturnal silence, one sound would
Break it, lulling me to sleep:
The J-Train, rolling on light rail train tracks
On the hill, in back of my townhouse.
Easy to feel those wooden floor vibrations.
Soothing enough to listen & pass out to.
The J-Train on its rounds, every 15 minutes:

Moving west, outbound, Balboa Park
Moving east, inbound, Embarcadero
Iron track lullaby—

W: 6.10.14

CONDOS

October 2003:

14th & Guerrero:

Over the fence,
Up the scaffold,
Peeling plastic wrap
And duct tape off a
New window & opening it
Gently, I made my way into
A condo, built but not quite
Finished, where I'd unrolled my
Sleeping-bag & rested for 12 nights.
In before midnight. Out by sunrise.

23rd & Harrison:

Black canvas
Covered scaffolds
That blended well with the night
Made my job of entering
New condos hella easy.
I took the stairs to the 4th floor.
Found a room, a blind spot in
This work-in-progress to rest in,
Smelling of sheetrock dust & fresh lumber.
Before bedtime, I visited
The rooftop terrace, some snob's
Future patio, and in the open air, my eyes
Paid greetings to the full, pale moon
Over the shadow of Bernal Hill
And the myriad lights of my new city.

W: Father's Day 2014

BLACK STAR

August 2004:

My energy was spent
On Modesto's streets,
Joining friends in
Their struggle to
Reclaim the parks
For the extremely poor on Saturday afternoon.

By sundown, Doug drove me to Sylvan Boulevard
And shown me up close
The nerve centre for the struggle:

A Copwatch meeting room,
A Food Not Jails cookhouse,
A donated clothing storehouse,
Anti-authoritarian infoshop,
Living quarters that had
No landowner. All in one.
My friends, its occupants,
Shared the space, shared the land.
Big pasture, creaky floorboards, spray-can
Anarchist graffiti on the walls.
Little black star
Never appeared on Modesto's map.
Autonomous zone
Liberated from a conservative city.

My biggest regret in entering:

Not wearing a face masque for protection
From the piss bucket's stench.

W: 6.20.14

THE TEAHOUSE

November 2, 2004:

Inside Arizona State's Gammage Auditorium:

Democrat—Republican
Senator—President
War veteran—War maker—
Before a live, attentive audience,
Both statesmen faced off.
Before CNN© cameras,
Staged opposition.
Before Election Day,
The last debate.

Outside Gammage Auditorium:

Young Democrats—Young Republicans
Disenfranchised—Privileged
"Stop the war"—"Stay the course"—
A crowd of anti-state demonstrators I joined
[With some Libertarians & Greens in the mix]
Did their best to bring the war to Tempe
And supporters of both Capitalist parties.
Disruption to the last great
Political clownshow inside, an insult to
Society's intelligence.

After the protest was over,
Like several nights before, I
Retired to the Teahouse on South Hardy Street,
On the roof, nestled in my sleeping-bag, head on tiny
Travel pillow, exposed to late-night desert chill,
Aeroplanes from Phoenix International Airport
Flew overhead, voyages to who knows where.
I dreamt of a possible, ideal world with
Neither Democrats nor Republicans nor
Libertarians nor Greens nor elections nor
Governments nor masters nor slaves.

W: 7.4.14

FORT DOOM

September 2005:

The Lower Haight
Was in a state
Mainly of slumber
And so was I.
Small, foldable Bulova travel
Alarm clock rang me
Awake at 6am.

Another day began. I arose & would
Fill the red & black AK® Press bag with
Textbooks, notebooks, pens & a couple
Circle-A pamphlets,
Fill the Jansport® until bursting with a
Change of black clothes, full soap dish, toothbrush,
Toothpaste, deodourant stick, white towel, white
Wash cloth, lotion, hand sanitiser, black Kiwi®
Shoe polish [the liquid kind] before strapping it
On my back. I'd left my clean, dark
Windowless room with candles, sleeping, floorbound
Squatmates, Oak Street flat behind, out the
Basement side door to face the day. J-Train on
Church Street carried me straight to
City College, Ingleside main campus—
Shower, dry & dress in gymnasium men's locker room,
Breakfast at campus cafeteria, 3 classes,
Lunch at Ananda Fuara, homework at Rosenberg
Library, wash clothes at coin-op launderette,
Drop off my black Dickies® jacket at cleaners,
Dinner at Herbivore, Death Guild on Monday night,
Protest the U.S. military invasion of Iraq every night,

Return home to darkness & racket
From train-hopping, hitchhiking, spare-changing
Hardcore Punk youth who gave our
Home its unusual, warlike name—

Never mind Punk Rock.
Squatting saved my ass.

W: 7.22.14

CASA ZAPATISTA

July 2007:

Leftover property from the Mission District's
Irish-Catholic days, smack
On the corner of Harrison & 20th. Desolation central.

Ground floor: Home to
Rusty, dusty, cobwebbed Mexican/Salvadorean
Restaurant equipment & furniture.
It still stank of grease & pupusas.

Top floor: One bedroom,
Rattrap apartment, bare as
Anna Nicole Smith's head used to be.

La Casa, named in honour of Chiapas'
Mexican Indian warriors against globalisation,
Graced by my presence twice:

The first: Jonah, Kim & I entered through the back door.
In the midnight darkness, this skinny Tenant's Union
Counselor woman & I spoke of our lives. Then the
Three of us slept beside each other on the hardwood floor.
Upon awakening, Kim & I shared our first
Awkward hug.

The last: One Sunday morning, Jonah took off
Prior to my waking up.
The White building owner caught me
Stepping out of the bathroom.
The angry landlord gave me two options:
Leave that apartment in 5 minutes
Or he would start dialing 9-1-1 on his cellphone.

I vacated that rattrap in less than 5 minutes.
Out of pity for my living situation,
The landlord handed me $10 on the way out, to
Get something to eat. Great idea.
Blueberry pancakes & peppermint tea
At Brainwash provided me with
A delicious ending to my squatting episode.

W: 7.30.14

Feed

This ain't no charity.
This is a protest.

Supermarkets, hotels,
Eateries, coffeeshops
Make waste out of fresh & prepared
Food, tonnes, by day's end.

This ain't no church function.
This is a protest.

Bullets, assault rifles, tanks,
Aeroplanes, destroyer ships, bombs
Make far-away lands killing fields.
National budget spent mostly on this, forget homes.

This ain't no city programme.
This is a protest.

Hunger tends to exist
In the First World, too.
So food is recovered
From rotting as waste.

This ain't no welfare line.
This is a protest.

Ongoing against military build-up.
Gearing up for war, nights and days
Dining from empty plates, drinking from empty cups,
Sleeping on empty bellies, dreaming of a decent meal.

Revolution sometimes begins from
The bottom of a bowl.
Public space gets reclaimed.
That space becomes inclusive.
Fresh, prepared, free
Vegetarian food is shared with neighbours.

Afterwards, workers & poor alike leave

The corner with fuller bellies.
Hunger is much worse on the streets.
So some do what class society fails to do:

Feed the people.
Food to every fork.

This ain't no charity.
This is a protest.

W: 12.5.14

That
which
is
empty
&
unused,
make
it
yours.

About Dee Allen.

Dee Allen is an African-Italian performance poet based in Oakland, California. Active on creative writing & Spoken Word since the early 1990s. Author of 9 books—*Boneyard, Unwritten Law, Stormwater, Skeletal Black* [all from POOR Press], *Elohi Unitsi* [Conviction 2 Change Publishing], *Rusty Gallows* [Vagabond Books], *Plans* [Nomadic Press], *Crimson Stain* [EYEPUBLISHEWE] and *Discovery* [Southern Arizona Press]—and 72 anthology appearances under his figurative belt so far. To date, *The Mansion* is his 10th book.

Print Appearances

"Beneath" *Poor Magazine*, March 29, 2012.

"Beneath" *Indybay*, Thursday March 22, 2012.

"Hoody" *Poor Magazine,* March 29, 2012.

"Homecoming" *Political Affairs*, November 18, 2012.

"Disembark" *Poets 11: 2012,* Friends Of The San Francisco Public Library, 2013.

"Ella Hill Hutch" *Out Of Our #14*, September 10, 2012.

"Standstill" *Overthrowing Capitalism*. Kallatumba Press, 2014

"Standstill" *Indomitable #4*, December 30, 2012.

"Wooden Cello" *Riverbabble #27*: Summer 2015.

"The Mansion" *Colossus: Home,* Colossus Press, 2020 [Excerpt— Part 10].

"Stay Silent" *Tides Of Flame #24*, Early November 2012

"Stay Silent" *Revolutionary Poets Brigade*, Wednesday November 7, 2012.

"Ghost Dance" *The Contributor*. January 31 – February 13, 2013

"Ghost Dance: *Political Affairs,* January 10, 2013 [Last Section/Chorus 2 Omitted]

"Ghost Dance" *Homeward Street Journal*, March-April 2013.

"Invertebrate" *Fireworks #2*, Summer 2013

"Invertebrate" *Indybay*, Friday July 5, 2013.

"The Thorn" *Impact: Personal Portraits Of Activism*, Musewrite, 2020 [Excerpt—Part 4].

"Ambassadors" *Denver Voice*. June 2014.

"Ambassadors" *Homeward Street Journal,* March-April 2014

"Ambassadors" *Street Sheet*, September 2015.

"Shining Star" *Poets 11: 2014*, Friends Of The San Francisco Public Library, 2015.

"Derelict 2" *Homeward Street Journal*, July-August 2014.

"Feed" *The Challenger*, November 2016.

"Feed" *Street Sheet*, January 2015.

"Feed" *Poetry X Hunger*, May 10, 2020.

"Feed" *Patrice Lumumba: An Anthology Of Writers On Black Liberation*, Nomadic Press, 2021.

Appendix
In Order of Appearance

ATL - Abbreviation for "Atlanta"

Dirty Dirty - Atlanta Hip Hop community slang for The Southern United States

The Dirty Dog - My nickname for the Greyhound bus

Ella Hill Hutch - Community centre located in San Francisco's historically Black Fillmore District. Named in honour of the first Black female San Francisco county supervisor [1977-1981] and Bay Area Rapid Transit Board of Directors member [1974-1977]

CATS - Community Awareness & Treatment Services: A houseless advocacy group in San Francisco

MUNI - San Francisco Municipal Railway

SRO - Single Room Occupancy

"The Real Bettie Page" - A biography book on the life of 1950s swimsuit/fetish model Bettie Page. The 2006 film "The Notorious Bettie Page" was based on this book.

UDR - United Dominion Realty, based in Pleasanton, California

Wasi'chu - LAKOTA "Greedy people." Used to describe European (White) settlers & the Army

Shunkawakan - LAKOTA "Horses." Literal translation: "Great dogs."

Turbinado - Raw Hawai'ian cane sugar. Also called "blond sugar" or "Sugar In The Raw"

PNAC - Project for a New Amerikkkan Century, a Neo-Conservative group that consisted of members of President George Bush's Cabinet. The object of Gulf War 2: "full spectrum dominance" [U.$. political/military control of the Middle East]

B.A.R.T. - Bay Area Rapid Transit

P.G.&E. - Pacific Gas & Electric

E.B.T. - Electronic Benefits Transfer

Jayhawks - Kansas University's football team & mascot. Used here as a term to describe K.U. students

Sweat Equity - Value in a property that results from the work that a person does to improve it

Zuni's - High-priced Italian & French restaurant

Kawaida - SWAHILI: "Tradition". Afrocentric thought.

Death Guild - San Francisco's oldest Darkwave/EBM club night since 1993. Currently at DNA Lounge.

Brainwash - A combination coffeeshop, launderette & dry cleaners, located at 7th & Folsom Streets in San Francisco's South Of Market neighborhood. Now closed down.

Praise for The Mansion

Dee Allen's collection of poems and song lyrics flesh out his premise that "Not every mansion is a playground for the wealthy." Within this book, he shares his experiences in the world of the homeless, hungry, disenchanted and dispossessed. In his poem "Standstill", he echoes Mario Savio, free speech warrior, suggesting the only way to halt the cruelties of capitalism is to jam up the cogs through passive resistance and shut down the machine. Other poems speak of social justice, articulating a vision of a sustainable alternative where "anyone can partake from what collective work ushered in: the growing green future freed from asphalt and the grasp of landlords." In "Hoody" he calls out white privilege for the lethal toll it takes on black lives, specifically Trayvon Martin. His title poem, *The Mansion*, rendered as a series of journal entries, is a powerful chronicle detailing squats, busts, stubborn persistence. He concludes with a call to feed the hungry, claim the unused—this is how to survive.

Dr. Jennifer Lagier Fellguth, author of *Weeping in the Promised Land* and managing editor of Monterey Poetry Review

The ongoing crisis of homelessness and the broken systems our unhoused communities are dependent upon gets a long overdue insiders' perspective in Dee Allen's brilliant *The Mansion*, an essential and brutally honest collection of personal poems and song lyrics. A long admired and passionate poet, Allen uses his storyteller skills to illustrate what living a locked out, chained out life is really like. Suffering erratic housing, squatting in abandoned buildings owned by hostile landlords, treated like a criminal despite having committed no crime... Dee Allen's *The Mansion* looks squarely at the people experiencing homelessness with grace, respect and loving compassion.

James Cagney, author of *MARTIAN: The Saint of Loneliness*, 2021 winner of the James Laughlin Award from Academy of American Poets

The Mansion is a collection of witness statements which opens the veil on those who we would rather not see, the homeless. Dee Allen speaks of "Keeping the invisible poor quite invisible." He teaches us: "You have good intentions, // Good for you." He shows us who they are: "Never mind Punk Rock. // Squatting saved my ass." Every piece shows us the truth of our shared humanity with the wit, kindness, and courage which makes the truth of our shared failure as a nation worth the discomfort of knowing.

Donald Krieger, Poet, biomedical researcher, co-host of *Cultivating Voices* open mic, author of *When Danger Is Past, Who Remembers?*

Some of the poems in *The Mansion* I've heard before. Powerful presentations from Dee Allen, borne on his magnificent voice. Reading this collection of his poems, set into a context and a chronology, brings a cumulative comprehension of the poetry, drawing the reader into Dee's life and spirit—his means of survival, his political nuance, his sense of adventure.

Mary Susan Gast, Poet, Human Rights Advocate